NOT A WORD WAS WRITTEN

NOT A WORD WAS WRITTEN

AMIT KUMAR MALL

ZORBA BOOKS

Published in India by Zorba Books, 2017

Website: www.zorbabooks.com
Email: info@zorbabooks.com

Copyright © Amit Kumar Mall

Translated by Deepak Chaudhary

ISBN Print Book : 978-93-86407-03-0
ISBN eBook : 978-93-86407-04-7

All rights reserved. No part of this book may be reproduced or transmitted in any form or by any means, electronic or mechanical, including photocopying, recording, or by an information storage and retrieval system—except by a reviewer who may quote brief passages in a review to be printed in a magazine, newspaper, or on the Web—without permission in writing from the copyright owner.

Although the author and publisher have made every effort to ensure the accuracy and completeness of information contained in this book, we assume no responsibility for errors, inaccuracies, omissions, or any inconsistencies herein. Any slights on people, places, or organizations are unintentional.

Zorba Books Pvt. Ltd.(opc)
Gurgaon, INDIA

Printed at : Repro Knowledgecast Limited, Thane

Dedicated to

**My grand mother Late Tilakraji Kuwari
And
My grand father, Late Ganesh Mall**

Foreword

<u>For A Great Tomorrow To Look Forward To</u>
Anand Prakash

The book 'Not A Word Was Written' contains Amit Kumar Mall's poems in English translation; these were originally written in Hindi and the collection came out in 2002 as 'Likha Nahin Ek Shabd'. Rendered in English by Deepak Chaudhry, these poems offer a taste of Mall's poetry for the benefit of readers not conversant with Hindi. I would gladly recommend these poems to the sane and intelligent reader ever in search of articulation of what s/he is confronted with in the prevailing ethos. It can indeed be pronounced that socio-cultural practice in our midst has made a mincemeat of all we hold dear in our surroundings, be it values of solidarity, love, tolerance, equality, or that vision of harmonious togetherness that is gradually weakening and is threatening to finally disappear from the scene we have. I noted unmistakably the pain the poet felt all along his path of creativity as he evolved as a vigilant observer of life's details. Consider that this sentiment of pain was felt almost a decade and a half ago but it has joined well, sadly, with what we spot today, and to which Mall's recently published collection of Hindi poems 'Phir' (kindly provided by the poet along the present manuscript for me to read) testifies.

For making a few points, let me begin with a short quote from this book. "Breath may not/ Accompany you till the end,/ Fight to/ Initiate to fight ... Fight for the dream of/ Fighting" (6). This leads us to the stances Mall assumes in the act of composition. Lines such as these are hard to pass by in a poetry collection where subtle insights interact to become a perspective of hope. One is witness here to a mind at once daring and thoughtful—something rare in the current literary scene; in general, poets are ever so habituated to say the obvious and rest content there. Instead, Mall remains gently persuasive. His aim is to share with the reader experiences rooted in our surroundings; these receive from his sensibility quiet verbal touches.

As I read along, the poems wove a lyrical pattern. They were independent and apart from one another, taking into their fold scattered elements of a disparate world. Soon, however, they aligned mutually to become a creative viewpoint of questioning. The poet is equipped with a framework of values and judges with its help the negative features of the surroundings. His lyricism is smooth on one side, whereas on the other it is disturbingly alert and demanding. Not for him the idealistic stance of supposedly high talk or of preaching the trite. Instead, he believes in complicating issues—"I am Rama,/ I am Vibhishana, / I am Bharata,/ And I am Ravana,/ I can't escape." The question takes a turn to become—"I wished to feel,/ But got involved in/ Weaving hatred,/ Performing tasks,/ Making name." Further, the poet's 'I' is confronted with issues of the given life:

In a December night
Inside a tattered blanket,
In an unsullied piece of attire
Offering shelter to a child
Crying on the footpath,
In the death of graying dreams of
A youth.

Apparently mundane, the scene brings to notice the denial of sustenance to a large chunk of our population. Cries of the child and defeated dreams of youth can shake anyone but the cold-hearted. Poets cannot wax eloquent on the country's heritage and achievements of a few individuals; they have keep their eyes and ears open to troubles rampant in contemporary conditions. This forms the backdrop of all poems in the collection.

The first part of poem collection covers a vast arena and probes the question of link between the 'I' of the poem and the surrounding world; the latter has many shades of reality to offer, soft and sweet as well as hard and daunting. Yet, the 'I' looks in wonderment at the spectacle of constructed beauty in the surroundings. On one side is city-centric existence of harmony and on the other the effort-driven routine of the peasant carrying plough on his shoulder to the fields. The sweat and grime of life makes the poet raise doubts about the world he lives in. He sees in this many possibilities of peace and rhythm, but is not sure though if those indeed would be realized; there seem no indications of fulfillment in a picture that is ridden with poverty, inequality and want. The reader may see bafflement of the poetic voice out to secure equanimity or stability in vain. Each section of the poem probes the issue from a new angle to eventually end in the larger helplessness.

There are answers to the problematic phenomenon in vague suggestions — they belong to the realm of expectation. It is heartening that the poet is laying stress all across the poem on the might of creative imagination even as the tone is kept mild and suggestive. Pointers to resolution emanating from such a representation range from "No matter if/ Victory eludes you,/ Just fight to put up/ A tough fight"(6) through "Many times,/ I set out, but/ Got exhausted, trapped/ In locks of hair,/ In pleasure,/ In my own grief" (9) to "The world, if it stays on,/ Then it must be such that/ You alone may write your fate,/ Your tears may blossom into smiles,/ Your labour may bear/ The smell of honour and respect" (17). We note that "honour" and "respect" remain the guiding principles of human endeavour resting upon energythe creative mind would generate. Is the poet finding little in the contemporary ethos for inspiration? The issue gets raised poignantly. We are reminded of the opening lines of the sequence that laid a plan to gaze upon prospects of viewing a world difficult to comprehend:

A mask has come
On the face
That does not laugh
And does not cry either,
Not a word was owned.

The mask symbolizes the poetic effort of a mind out to make sense of the present scenario; it has not much to make the viewer laugh, nor induce him to sadly watch the unfolding drama before his eyes. More, the face shows signs of going completely dumb. What to say, which stance to adopt? The parts of the long poem, linking up with one another and yet retaining their identity make a statement about events that happen in our times. They apparently stay distant and give the impression of making comments of limited scope about today's life.But wait, the poet has something larger to depict; these apparently stray impressions combine to reflect a trend of hope

inherent in each case.
A philosophical view informs the poem in question, it talks of lyrical substance floating far back in the horizon to which the poet has tied himself emotionally. One is made conscious of a Tagore-like vision of unity between the mundane and the platonic, and the reader is reassured that the world in our time may have gone off tangent, but steadiness of purpose is not far away from its boundaries. Interestingly, this cannot be said about the next set of poems which constitute the parameter of disillusionment. Is the poet gaining in breadth and constructing for himself a pattern of realistic appraisals?

The poems in the next section, They are aphoristic and assertive. Instead of sharing an experience with the reader, they seek to state and tell. To go further, these poems disturb the reader into a state of watching with horror the developments that have left the poet unnerved, if not altogether shattered. See the way the poet decides to call the existing picture a moment in the frame of larger time, and squeezes into the tiny details a broad array of tumultuous episodes:

Time turned into
A frantic squall, and
Passed by blowing.
I kept flurrying
Sheets of paper
Piled up before me.

We are face to face here with Time becoming a squall and in consequence the poet-persona witnessing it frozen in words on paper. What should the reader make of it? Should s/he apply the observation to the existing scene and draw lessons from it useful for determining a role for self? I believe this to be the case since Mall's intent is to etch a line deep enough in the reader's mind—it will not be erased unless serious steps are taken to address the malady. For the poet, the phenomenon is of an upheaval involving shake-up of existence on a high scale. We are not allowed to ask as to how such a thing happened and who was answerable for causing it in the first place. Clearly, it conveys the mood of present-day reality.

Barring a few, the short poems under this category of evocative statements relate well to the events we are witness to in our own time; they address concrete issues in the format of impressions theyhave left on the poet's reactive mind. The poems touchthe sense of closure and a stasis as if the imagination active so far is eventually giving up. Mark the poem 57 for the mental state the poet is in. He says, "Don't clash with truth/ Deliberately/ If you have to lead a life,/ Foster a fanciful confusion/ For yourself." In the existing scenario, feels the poet, it is difficult to make sense of the ideal one finds worth preserving. For this reason, he considers that fancy alone is the thing; in fact, the case is made still more difficult by "confusion" because of which using fancy itself has become a futile venture. I call this dilemma precious. Few will venture to grasp a situation going against the grain of the system we chose to pursue. Significantly, even as the poet admitted defeat, its articulation drew attention to factors responsible for the said defeat. The outer world sought to halt the truth and conversely, the sense of meaning was born as the human being engaged in fight. The penultimate poem expresses the conundrum well: "Don't deceive me,/ Dreams! I am wounded./ Be the prologue to/ Whatever comes on my way." For the poet, dreams show the way out of the stalemate eventually. We have a poet with us raising questions of poetic expression caught in the twists of ideological-emotional engagement.

In the book, we come across a third poetic variant. This indicates initial impressions in the longer first poem consisting of the many small parts and those latter ones where pithiness of expression is key. Here, lyricism is put to use as the poet experiments with a form pursued and made famous by Tagore in Gitanjali. When Tagore wrote his songs in early twentieth century, times were filled with passion for the new that was greatly inspiring. Also, Tagore's engagement was with nature—the storm, the sea, the child and those areas of passion innate in the human being. When Amit Kumar Mall is writing, the mood is of pain, defeated ideals, bitterness and disappointment. Giving nature the go by, Mall turns towards longing and melancholy. We discern in Mall a feeling of sad reflection permeating the songs. In one respect, these songs join with the aphoristic short, four- or five-liners numbering 53 in the preceding section. It is the bitter ironical tone coming through in each case. In these poems, the addressee is primarily a woman figure haunting imagination and evoking indulgence, rejection and detachment in one go. These combine to become an acceptance of what went on for some time but failed at the end. To quote: "This hand is empty now/ In the sea of sands,/ Thorns have grown/ On my barren palms./ Belle! How would I/ Take your attire under my care?". Read it together with "We don't come across humans/ On earth now,/ Bring spirits from somewhere,/ I am broken, dispersed, scattered here and there,/ Pals! String into tears the pearls of my being/ Before I sink", and see the spread and expanse the poet is able to achieve. Indeed, at one level the poet has moved on from moments of involvement in an experience, yet at another he is looking back for support that may come from the ones near him. He hopes that the friends will listen and be with him when he is "broken, dispersed, scattered."

From here, we may further go to a view of cold judgment and self-revival. The last in the series is the statement of sad admission that surroundings have lost glitter and draw notice only as dissipated entities:

Crowd is thickening at the crossroads,
The path would now be more solitary.

and

Man has discovered numerous means of death,
Life would find itself trapped in more difficulty.

In this series of song-like compositions, I observe a preoccupation with the world the poet lives in; he is not rejecting it to go off on a separate plane of existence but cannot appreciate the given logic of the world either. What does one do? Mall leaves it to the reader to ponder over. His sharing of feelings, honest and forthright, is indictment enough of the state of affairs we have. The poet's response to existing challenges is deeply human and rational, leaving little to the realm of pious hopes. Still, sharing gives space to the reader to think. Much may thus depend on how our society's sensitive sections respond to Amit Kumar Mall's poetic endeavour.

I am sure the poems in this volume will appeal to the

English-knowing reader raising for her/him existential and ideological points as well those other subjects that alert one in terms of authenticity and honesty. There is a large readership of young people in the country eager to know about and grapple with contentious parameters of suffering humanity spread across the social spectrum. The humanity I talk of is of the destitute making do with meager resources, the helpless middle class facing crisis of ideals, and intelligentsia deciphering codes of myth, tradition, and folklore. Without being prescriptive, one may expect poetry of this variety to gain further in detail, information and depth to cover segments such as women, the socially oppressed at the level of suffering, deprivation and neglect. All these qualify for attention from courageous literary voices. Amit Kumar Mall is one such name to figure prominently in the list of writers having a great tomorrow to look forward to.

Anand Prakash
Retd. Head of Deptt, English Deptt,
Hansraj College, Delhi University,
E-mail id : anand1040@gmail.com

Preface

I started my literary journey in the year 1982 , when my first article was published in a Hindi weekly magazine, Saptahik Hindustan. My first book of poems in hindi entitled. 'Likha Nahi Ek Shabd' , was brought out in 2002.

Aptly titled , 'Not a Word was Written', this book is the English rendering of my first anthology of poems , 'Likha Nahi Ek Shabd'. It goes without saying that English is the global language of communication today. Therefore, reaching out to readers, who are thoroughly acquainted with, and have a creative understanding of English language is a dream that almost every writer of our age cherishes. My case is no exception in this regard

I am pleased to see that the English translation of my book has brought me so close to realizing this dream. I am thankful to Mr. Deepak Chaudhary for his sincere and painstaking endeavor to produce this English translation. The introduction to this book was written by the noted scholar Mr. Anand prakash, retired HOD, Department of English , Hansraj College , University of Delhi . I am very grateful to him for his generous and morale boosting willingness to introduce the book to the community of English speaking literary and reading gentry across the globe. I also extend my gratitude to Mr. Ambika Nand Sahay, former resident editor, The Times of India, for his valuable comment. I express my thankfulness to Prof. Chandan kumar, University of Delhi, Mr. Umesh k. Singh, editor, the Times of India news web-site, Mr. Pradeep Singh, assistant professor, Delhi university, Prof. Pankaj Kumar, Allahabad University, Mr. Ramendar Singh, lecturer in Delhi govt and Shubhra Dubey, research scholar, Centre for English Studies, Jawaharlal Nehru University, for their invaluable help and support in publishing of this book . I am also thankful to Zorba books for publishing this book and thus paving the way for a part of my creative oeuvre to access the reading gentry worldwide. At this moment, I also want to thank. my wife Neeta and my two sons, Akshay and Akshat for their indirect support.

I hope that the book will be well by readers

Thank you

Amit Kumar Mall

CONTENTS

1. Days went by — 23
2. If you want to identify me — 25
3. Bruised to the backbone — 26
4. Why do you weigh my strength to fight — 27
5. Scattering — 28
6. Fight — 29
7. Is it an impact of aging ? — 30
8. I put down the Gandeeva — 32
9. Many times I went out — 33
10. Time! — 35
11. Charming visage — 36
12. The battle is on — 37
13. Which door should — 38
14. I know — 40
15. Psyche! Take me — 43
16. Pausing on — 45
17. If this world alone — 47
18. Somewhere — 48
19. Life ! Standing at your threshold — 49
20. In turns — 50
21. The pictures — 51
22. After serving — 52

23. The way of life	53
24. I work for eons	54
25. Where there is life	55
26. Sorrow melting, thawing	56
27. It's a	57
28. Who has	58
29. Time turned into	59
30. If you have to	60
31. I stopped	61
32. At the city's crossroads	62
33. Amidst all	63
34. Gods! Please don't take away	64
35. Life! Don't hold	65
36. Don't be surprised to see	66
37. I saw humans	67
38. This world of umpteen wonders will	68
39. Paint it	69
40. I bow down	70
41. I was a soldier who	71
42. Of this earth	72
43. I was just dead, when	73
44. I did not initiate	74
45. Good opportunity	75
46. In the storm of	76
47. I kept reading	77
48. Why should I gaze at	78
49. Before throwing a stone	79

50. Locked into a race for survival	80
51. If you don't think of me	81
52. I am fond too	82
53. Please don't	83
54. In every face	84
55. Arrival of spring is	85
56. Turning the world into paradise by	86
57. Don't clash with truth	87
58. One must be familiar with	88
59. You are unfaithful but	89
60. I am not God	90
61. I have seen	91
62. The hell will not	92
63. Spirits don't visit	93
64. A few stones fell	94
65. Stop playing	95
66. Same companion	96
67. Many people you come across	97
68. Keep meeting people	98
69. Don't deceive me	99
70. Life is a game of destinies	100
71. Pal! Why do you test me	101
72. A man is never indeed a man	103
73. I have found the world in your eyes	104
74. In a city of stones	106
75. I would smile a lot, but	107
76. In solitudes	108

77. Tomorrow	109
78. I don't want wine	111
79. Though I am moist with	113
80. Dear belle! How would I see	114
81. I have liked	116
82. Life! I am very happy	118
83. Bring down fairies and nymphs	120
84. Stop if you can	121
85. Inflict more pain	122
86. We are mausoleums of	123
87. Everybody wonders	125
88. Laugh, smile	126
89. The heart is sinking in sadness	127
90. The fragrance	128
91. Come along, let's go somewhere	129
92. O Lord! Take some pity	131
93. I am a heart of glass	132
94. Let me breathe in the open air	133
95. I have no trust in myself	134
96. I grayed moment by moment	135
97. Quest for humans	136
98. In the ambiance of void	137
99. In this era	138

1.

Days went by,
Not a word was written

There was ink,
There were eyes, open and awake
But not a word was written

There were sensitivities,
Tongues were not tied,
But not a word was spoken

There is grief
And a reason too, to feel aggrieved,
But not a word was borne

Man now
Appears to be a crowd,
Not a word was lived

Spread of the firmament
Became confined within me,
Not a word was filled

A mask has come
On the face
That does not laugh

And does not cry either,
Not a word was owned

2.

If you want to identify me,
Then look at
The chirping bird of dawn

If you want to identify me,
Then look at
The searing-shimmering spark

If you want to identify me,
Then look at
The seeds dissolving in earth
And sprouting

I will emerge
Bursting out of petrified soil
Where barrenness blooms
Amidst thorny copses

3.

Bruised to the backbone,
Soul wounded,
A whimper groaning,
Wailing, dawdling from earth to sky,
But I am not defeated

Frailty sparkles through the eyes,
Shaky arms,
Quiver broken apart,
Evanescing, faded aspirations,
But I am beating, and will
Keep beating as I do

O masters of time!
I am pausing not to
Ease my breath,
But to overcome my exhaustion
And stitch my sores

I will be back!
I will be back again
To fight this battle,
This battle alone

4.

Why do you weigh my strength to fight
From the lines on my back?

Why do you test the pitch of my voice
From my muteness?

Why do you test the strength of my arms
From my loose fists?

Why do you test the extremes of my pain
From the depth of my wounds?

Friend!
Don't test the fire of volcano
From its silence
From the equanimity of a sea,
Don't test its tempest
If you test the strength of this spark,
Your world will incinerate

5.

Scattering,
Slipping...
I bound the letters,
Closed my fists
And caught the words

I lent them meanings,
Underpinnings,
I gave them feelings
With a fiery blaze

Words, once they
Had an identity,
Began to deviate,
Veer away from set patterns,
They began to know themselves
From the new meanings
They assumed

6.

Fight
To win
Without giving in

No matter if
Victory eludes you,
Just fight to put up
A tough fight

Breath may not
Accompany you till the end,
Fight to
Initiate a fight

No matter if
There is no beginning,
Fight for a conviction in
The spirit of fighting

Till your conviction thaws,
Turning into
A molten block of ice,
Fight for the dream of
Fighting

7.

Is it
An impact of aging?
Some temporary halt in
Life's journey?
A patch of frustration? Or,
Some compromise?
I can't say.

Truth is what
Lies before me,
Truth is that
I can't fight.

It's fine if
You are there
But it's fine as well if
You aren't,
I can't wish.

Love, hatred,
Affection, disgust,
Selfishness ...
Whatever it is,
I can't avoid

I am Rama,
I am Vibhishana,
I am Bharata,
And I am Ravana,
I can't escape

8.

I put down
The Gandeeva

Pity in
The sheath of
Frailties

Who all
Should I fight with?
On the faces of my foes,
I see my own countenance

In Kurukshetra,
Arjuna is spineless,
Krishna is neutral,
Gandeeva is forceful but restricted,
I have to fight my battle
On my own

9.

Many times I went out,
But stopped with
My family,
In the world,
On the moral-spiritual fulcrum

Many times,
I set out, but
Got exhausted, trapped
In locks of hair,
In pleasures,
In my own grief

I wished to feel,
But got involved in
Weaving hatred,
Performing tasks,
Making name

In a December night
Inside a tattered blanket,
In an unsullied piece of attire
Offering shelter to a child
Crying on the footpath,

In the death of graying dreams of
A youth
I found you,
O my country,
I found you!

10.

Time!
Be a sea
Or a cascade

I will not be drowned
Even while flying
On the tides
Along restive currents

Like a straw,
I will come back
To float through
The next sea

11.

Charming visage,
Bewitching eyes,
Wanton chuckles,
Seductive gestures and
Mannerisms arouse
Amorous sensations,
Suggesting dappled fancies

Is this beauty or….. ?
This is medal that
Clings only
To the chest of
Competence

12.

The battle is on

The fire of the belly is
Doused with sweat and
Corns on the hands,
Battle between hunger
And bread is on

The body needs bread,
And for bread alone
The body sells itself,
Battle between shame and
Compulsion is on

With buds,
Thorns also grow
On plants,
Battle to bloom is on
With the ambiance

13.

Which door should
I knock,
Which thoroughfare should
I pause in, and call out?
Each gush of wind in
This city is deaf

My mirror is scared,
Dumbstruck
In the siege of voices,
Shaking, shouting, shuddering,
Who should I call? Who??
On the mirror of this city,
No face emerges anywhere

Life is fighting amidst
Stammering voices,
How long can I go on calling,
Yearning for a company
In this city of muted breaths

In this city of
Petrified silence,
I will knock at the doors

To make the dead souls hear me,
I will call at the crossroads,
I will keep calling till
The voice stays alive!!

14.

I know
Buds don't smile
In a scorching noon of June,
In the grab of a simmering loo

I know
The dagger that pierced me
Came from the wall
Against which I had reclined,
While running around, exhausted,
Anxious for a safe refuge

Shuffling, scampering, escaping
Sands offer glimpses of water,
But water, the real water
Remains elusive, untraceable

Stick to the truth,
Stand at the fulcrum of
Morals, and yet fighting
Brings in no victory
Despite all your toil,
And all your good intents,
You lose every time,

Finding yourself at the
Receiving end,
Alone, hapless, unsupported

I know
An ambiance of hopelessness
Fosters nothing but
Melancholy

I know
Defeat is not only defeat,
But an injury to
Self-belief, a sore
Rankling in the heart
And in the mind

I also know
A man fights with currents,
But loses his battle
To the shores

That is why
You keep quiet,
Trapped in a tacit melancholy,
Crying

In defeat,
Laughter also gets defeated,
Freshness also loses

And so does joy

You be defeated,
And cry,
Cry more and more
If the psyche says,
Cry at the death of
Aspirations, cry
Even with a split self-belief,
But fight nevertheless,
Don't cease to fight,
In each breath of life
Fight, only fight

15.

Psyche! Take me
To that land where
There is no carnnival of fairies,
Where dawn has no monopoly
Over time,
Where there are no streams of
Joy everywhere

Where the world is
Not under the spell of

Benumbing ecstasy,
Where people don't indulge in
Tall talks,
Where dreams are not longer
Than nights

O psyche! Get back and take me
To where
There is no carnnival of fairies

Where there are barren farms,
Ploughshares,
Backs of the bullocks,
And shoulders of peasants

Amit Kumar Mall

Where there is love,
Quarrrel,
And entreaty,
O psyche! Take me to
That land where
There is no carnival of fairies

16.

Pausing on
The banks,
I ask myself why
I did not flow
With the flow

Which had motion,
Intrepidity, and
The company of time
Which had pleasure,
Fun and
Carelessness

Where there was
Someone's chest, there was
My scythe,
Where there was
My back, there was
Someone's knife,
There was no piety,
There was no sin

Sans an armour,
Hiding behind a wall,

Leaning against something
For respite,
I ask myself why
I am so worried, while
Watching houses
Flow away in flood,
Seeing someone pecking,
Poking at something with beaks

There is nothing like
Sin,
It's only a disparity of
Psyche and work,
Repenting,
The truth is only
Moving and flowing,
And flowing with motion,
Pace

17.

If this world alone
Has scripted their fate,
If their misfortune is
Written in destiny's hieroglyphs,
Their penury and haplessness
Are engraved on the stalagmites of
Destiny

If this alone is
The philosophy of the world
And existence, asserting that
Hunger and tears will
Come to them,
Then, o world! Change this philosophy
Or else, tears will turn into
Drops of blood

The world, if it stays on,
Then it must be such that
You alone may write your fate,
Your tears may blossom into smiles,
Your labour may bear
The smell of honour and respect

18.

Somewhere
There is a blind tunnel
That connects the world of books to
The world of ideals, and this tunnel
Opens nowhere!

19.

Life! Standing at your threshold
I feel,
What I read in books
Was written by
Some mad man

20.

In turns,
This is a journey of darkness
And light,
People who live it stitch the shreds,
Assemble the shards,
Aimlessly, in vain

21.

The pictures
That emerge with youth
Are now blurred,
They can't have a face
Sans bread,
The hope to stay alive

22.

After serving
The last man in the bar,
I also have a sip or two,
Yeah, I have committed
The sin too, of drinking and
Guiding others to
The pink trail

23.

The way of life
Was different for me,
I stood with uprightness,
And my existence
Went in smithereens

24.

I work for eons
And live for a day,
I take four births
To lead a life of four days

25.

Where there is life,
There is pain,
Everybody knows this
Age-old dictum, and
Yet never refrains from
Betting on life like a gambler

26.

Sorrow melting, thawing
Runs through each cell of
The body,
Tears keep flowing
At the shameless killing of
Conscience

27.

It's a
New custom of our age,
Zeitgeist…
Wars are waged for the sake of peace!

28.

Who has
Ever fought with time,
Destiny, God?
But the heart could not
Bear the haplessness of
The innocent child

29.

Time turned into
A frantic squall, and
Passed by blowing,
I kept flurrying
Sheets of paper
Piled up before me

30.

If you have to
Remain honest, serious, human,
Then go to a thoroughfare,
Some square, where
You can settle, sit, stay transfixed
Like a statue

31.

I stopped
Poking my head into
Mundane matters,
But the good wishes
Coming from pals
Did not let me live in peace

32.

At the city's crossroads,
I have been sitting
Motionlessly, guised as
An idol
Ever since I went away from
The territory of feelings
Such as affection,
Hatred,
Love

33.

Amidst all
That has been stated,
Heard and advised,
I make this announcement.
Don't ever discover my signs,
I have changed my shades

34.

Gods! Please don't take away
Sun from my courtyard,
I buried conscience
Yesterday only.

35.

Life! Don't hold
The winds blowing in
My house as hostage,
I have sealed my lips

36.

Don't be surprised to see
My wounds,
I used to stay in the company of
Buddies and friends

37.

I saw humans
As humans, and
Turned infidel, iconodule,
Life! Don't judge me by my
Style of worshipping,
It's just that
My way offering prayer is unique

38.

This world of umpteen wonders will
Meet the dust some day,
A letter that I am,
I will keep throbbing in the abyss
Like a microbe or a tiny molecule

39.

Paint it,
Sculpt it,
Close it in books,
My conscience is acid
That you will always find
Concentrated, extant

40.

I bow down
To every tower I come across,
God knows whose dagger is this
That has pierced so deep
Through the bosom

41.

I was a soldier who
Went down fighting,
They were bravehearts who
Went on counting the corpses

42.

Of this earth,
I was a tiny particle,
Wiped off in a bid to stop
The winds coming from outside
And minds placed cosily
In the capitals faraway,
Went on discussing the prospects of peace

43.

I was just dead, when
You laid so many flowers
On my tomb,
It seems you will
Never come back now

44.

I did not initiate
The war by stepping into
Your territory,
I only want the right
To die on the soil of this country

45.

Good opportunity,
Their gestures of grace,
My time...
I am lying in grave,
Come anyone! Come, wake me up,
Pull me out of my slumber

46.

In the storm of
Apprehensions,
Keep the candle of hope ignited,
Time is a frantic squall,
Sometimes blowing brown,
Sometimes slowing down

47.

I kept reading
The epitaph of time,
Fate kept turning into letters,
Permeating the text of life

48.

Why should I gaze at
The tides of success
My destination is
My path alone

49.

Before throwing a stone,
Sharpen it for sure
It's an era of propriety and
Correctness in manners

50.

Locked into a race for survival,
I kept braving allegations

Life! Throw a glance to this cranny too,
See how much fun fills in
Every inch of the abyss!

51.

If you don't think of me
As a friend,
Don't treat me as a
Foe either
It's not necessary to give
A name to every relation

52.

I am fond too,
Of propriety and discipline,
But when the heart is at stake,
It's hard to differentiate a river and a sea

53.

Please don't
Divide life into
Compartments of sorrow and joy
The age bygone
Has no name

54.

In every face,
I have tried to discover a man
Punish me,
My crime is grave

55.

Arrival of spring is
The talk of the town
I have seen blood in
The crimson mien of roses
That have bloomed

56.

Turning the world into paradise by
Making God out of everyone is
Acceptable,
But pray tell me where
I will get the joy of meeting you and
The pain of your separation

57.

Don't clash with truth
Deliberately
If you have to lead a life,
Foster a fanciful confusion
For yourself

58.

One must be familiar with
The proper way of living
There should be something
In the heart,
Something else in the eyes,
And something different
On the tongue

59.

You are unfaithful but
Why should I speak of
Solitudes?
I have got the company of
A broken heart,
Some dispersed tears,
Some half-baked feelings
And a quest

60.

I am not God
And so can't change the world
To me, it's acceptable
To burn to keep
Dark, dry faces shining

61.

I have seen
The truth underlying her tafetta temper
A mere glance of her
Can break a granite block
To smithereens

62.

The hell will not
Loose upon my head,
Even if you turn your eyes away
The heart that used to sing,
Would fall in silence

63.

Spirits don't visit
Crowded habitats
Call me
When you are in ruins

64.

A few stones fell
On my house yesterday
Some people have paid off
The debt they owed to me

65.

Stop playing
The game of scripting destinies
The crown is trampled, overrun,
When time changes

66.

Same companion,
Same moments,
Same tracks,
Same soirees
But when we meet,
Our tongues are silent
And eyes are moist

67.

Many people you come across
Will cry for you
Sometimes,
Shed a few drops for others

68.

Keep meeting people
Mirrors will show their faces

69.

Don't deceive me,
Dreams! I am wounded
Be the prologue to
Whatever comes on my way

70.

Life is a game of destinies,
What is to lose and what to find is
Immaterial
What was spent was good
And what has to come will
Bring in cries

71.

Pal! Why do you test me
Again and again?

I also walk on thorns like you,
I also gaze at the sun like you,
Pal! Why do you try my destiny
Again and again?

I was robbed exactly where
Your caravan had been raided,
I was wiped exactly where
You had been beheaded,
Pal! Why do you test my integrity
Again and again?

Dappled shade of buds
Pierces my sights too,
And when they bloom,
My heart also beats,
Pal! Why do you try my sensitivity
Again and again?

I also have to drink tears to laugh,
I also have to die frequently
To complete my life's graph,

Pal! Why do you test my verity
Again and again?

The silence of your city frightens me too,
Querying many times about my relations,
It quietens me too,
Pal! Why do you test my sagacity
Again and again?

I have also travelled in the company of hunger and thirst,
I have also confronted pain and crises at their worst,
Pal! Why do you test my identity
Again and again?

72.

A man is never indeed a man,
Somewhere less and somewhere he is the Lord of heaven

Out of the womb he comes only to reach the funeral ground,
And yet the seven seas are crossed by the man

Two meals and two yards of land amount to all he earns,
And yet he goes around projecting himself as
a superman

He avoids encountering his own self,
But with open arm does he meet others of his clan

Grappling with grief and countless obstacles,
He still keeps enquiring about tears' original stain

73.

I have found the world in your eyes,
I have found the world in your eyes

In your eyes, many seas whirl and flow,
In your eyes, many storms rise and blow,
I have found life in your eyes.

In your eyes, many chalices of wine hollow,
In your eyes, many sparks of lightning glow,
I have found the throb in your eyes.

When I listen to your eyes, my ears get the perfec rhyme,
When I read your eyes, heart is visible in its prime,
I have found a prayer in your eyes.

When I test your eyes, I can't say what I find,
The heart gets anxious, unleashing obsession undefined,
I have found an amorous fascination in your eyes.

Your eyes become a shadow accompanying me far and wide,
Your closed eyes touch mine and in proximity, our breaths collide,
I have found friendly affinity in your eyes.
Your eyes are light in my darkness,
Your eyes are remedy to my sickness

I have found the Almighty in your eyes,
I have found the world's entity in your eyes.

74.

In a city of stones, don't go carrying a glass heart,
Mix with all, but don't mix yours with any one's heart,
Smile at everything, but don't act like a piece of wax art,
Heart is just a piece of glass, don't let stones collide and tear it apart

Learn to feel the intimacy of your brethren,
Learn to trust in those who will give you pain,
Don't be surprised if the poison tastes sweet,
In this city of slayers, learn to be trapped in love and get slain.

In their hearts, never look for the sky's expansion,
Never try to see the sea's depths in their eyes veiled by pretension,
Don't talk to them about perishing for a faithful vow,
Today is yours, but for tomorrow, learn to live with your foe's disdain.

75.

I would smile a lot, but
Your dry eyes have dried up my smile.

I would fly in the sky, but
Your tied wings check my passion for flight.

I wish to feel exhilarated, but
But the stammer of your haplessness comes to mind.

People advise me to be happy, but
The pain of your heart makes me cry too.

My heart craves for great heights, but
How can I lose sight of my companions?

76.

In solitudes, one face emerges again and again,
Eyes looking down and shy countenance.

Sharp features and gestures mellow,
But beware! This is a killer's face.

Her laughter electrifies the surroundings with sparks,
Don't lose your senses, this is a narcotic cage.

77.

Tomorrow,
I will leave your city silently and go away,
'Love is a feeling', before departing
I will say.

If we ever meet anywhere,
In any lane of life ever,
I will look down and
Go away.

Tomorrow,
I will leave your city silently and Go away.
In the world of hunger and pain,
I had longed for you,
But leaving behind the relics of a rainbow fantasy,
Brused, wounded, I will go away.

Tomorrow,
I will leave your city silently and
Go away.

'I's so difficult
To maintain the bond of love',
Sharing this revelation with you,
I will say.

Tomorrow,
I will leave your city silently and
Go away.

78.

I don't want wine,
I am kicked all the way,
For better or for worse,
I am kicked all the way.

I am fired with zeal, passion
And the craze of youth,
My gestures are beyond parrallels,
I am kicked all the way.

Lost in someone's
Beauty and oomph,
I am beside myself without a drink,
Yeah, I am kicked all the way.

I course of journey, I laugh
And I cry too,
Neither decent, nor impudent,
I am kicked all the way.
In the muffling throes of
Loneliness, I die alone and Alone am I alive,
Solitudes! Don't call me, I am kicked all the way.

Some drops falling from
The eyes divest me of senses,

Wine bearer! Don't fill my glass,
I am kicked all the way.

79.

Though I am moist with
Teardrops frequently visiting my eyes,
Shower a trice of pain
So I can feel I am alive.

Tramps and nincompoops
Are rejected by all,
Reject my goodness
So I can feel I am alive.

Each hand yearns to
Gather flowers,
Gather thorns
So I can feel I am alive.

Everyone gets along,
Syncs with the life of pace,
Raise the fallen ones
So I can feel I am alive.

80.

Dear belle! How would I see
Your hands relishing the mehandi fair?

The mind gets dizzying shocks,
The head nears a split,
When the bowels are not filled,
I feel like burning within.

Belle! How would I
Comb your hair?

This hand is empty now
In the sea of sands,
Thorns have grown
On my barren palms.

Belle! How would I
Take your attire under my care?

The pain of this world
Gets down into my heart,
Poisoning my bosom
Sporadically.

Belle! How would I kiss
Your head, letting my heart go bare?

Fighting with the age,
My tongue and lips have dried,
Tired arms can't go up
To embrace you

Belle! My dear!
How would I make you my own
In life's tormenting affair?

81.

I have liked
And will like you for life,
Whether or not the tongue utters this,
But my eyes will keep looking at you for life,
I have liked
And will like you for life.

You don't know what
You are and what you aren't,
You don't know where
The head bowed in prayer,
I have adored
And will adore you for life.

Names that this annonymous entity
Has received from the world
Are incalculable,
I will become their fragrance
And smell for life.

Give the name of betrayal
To my faithfulness,
Try not to understand
My understanding, but

I will stick to what I have understood
For life

82.

Life! I am very happy,
Don't weigh this with my smile

I kept runnning around
To catch hold of shadows,
And have achieved everything,
Life! Don't see my glass to assess
My possessions

Expecting bright times in the offing,
I drank the venom of distress
To the core,
Life! Don't get carried away by my face,
Tears also fall in the excess of joy

Empathising with all,
Thinking of their pain as my own,
I have wiped tears from every face,
Life! Don't search for the traces of repute,
I am also included among the disreputed,
Bearing the indelible stain

I have observed
The world's every custom and rite,
But don't look for me in the crowd of faithfuls,

Life! There are limits beyond all this
And they are no less binding

At every defeat, I had celebrations
Just to keep each ray of hope alive,
Life! Please don't come in my dream
With a hope

83.

Bring down fairies and nymphs
From the sky,
Let's party together,
I am in the throes of grief, with
My each cell burnt to the hilt,
Pals! I am too thirsty, offer me a sea for drink

We don't come across humans
On earth now,
Bring spirits from somewhere,
I am broken, dispersed, scattered here and there,
Pals! String into tears the pearls of my being
Before I sink

Youth is going berserk with excitement,
Accelerating the heart-beat,
I am in the sky, flying, floating,
Bring me down for an earthy link

84.

Stop if you can,
Traveller! Quit the caravan
For a breathful of respite,
Leave the firmament
After all,
Time and destiny too are
Worldly illusions,
Adapt if you can,
Traveller! Give up even
The last straw of support
For fulfillment

85.

Inflict more pain,
Bring in a storm of distress,
The heart broken is not rent in smithereens,
A fulcrum is still left in a bit

Clean up your mirror more,
Some dust of confusion still stays on it,
Don't hide now and ever,
What you didn't really wish

The mind is shrouded in melancholy,
Silence is on the lips,
Cage the body more,
Some movement is still left in it

86.

We are mausoleums of
Faithfulness,
Fair mistress! Tread but somewhat gently,
Sway merrily, even with a swagger if you wish
But tread with a soft foot, gently

Heart and soul are laid out
On your path,
And we are all yours, but
Fair mistress! Tread somewhat gently

Bewitching charm of your gestures
Make the world swoon, collapse,
Spread it around,but
Fair mistress! Tread somewhat gently

Tying hair into a plait
Binds umpteen clusters of
Black, wanton couds,
Unlock it, spread it around if you wish, but
Fair mistress! Tread somewhat gently

It's not your fault if
People look and gaze at you,
The picture of you is fascinating, but

Fair mistress! Tread somewhat gently

The one who eventually woos
Your eyes, must be
The light of the divine,
But we have to kiss the earth only,
Fair mistress! Tread somewhat gently

87.

Everybody wonders
Why this man keeps so quiet,
Never groaning
Even while leading his life

Even with a barrage of injustice
Concealed within,
Why he keeps from
Calling his gods

Even after breaking
Like glass, why this man
Does not splinter,
Why he never extinguishes
Even in the reign of despair

Strange!! Strange is this man,
Who keeps smiling
Even when he is in pain,
And never breaks down
Even when he loses the game

88.

Laugh, smile,
Forget your grief,
Life is just a fun,
Enjoy it and depart

Faith is a rarity,
Don't seek for it here,
Move along, walk off with the one
Who promises company even for a yard

Pain is a sky,
You can find it everywhere,
Life is a burning flame,
Burn and depart

Why should we worry for tomorrow?
It's a myth,
Life is made of tiny, fleeting moments,
Enjoy it with full heart

Allegations will keep storming into Your territory,
Grievances will not cease to exist,
You can't address each one,
Do whatever your mind says
Before you depart

89.

The heart is sinking in sadness,
Come back if you can

For ages, I have been
Bearing the scorch of the rising sun,
Be an easterly and
Come back if you can

The dream of building everyone's world
Could not be realised,
But in case it may still be felt,
Come back if you can

I once wished to pluck the stars
And place at your feet,
Trust me,
Come back if you can

I can't change
The ways of the world,
Understanding the defeat of genuineness,
Come back if you can

90.

The fragrance
That smells all the time is
What the tongue calls affinity,
That which makes one feel tipsy without drink is
What the world calls love

Save me from the slanted sights of the age,
Hide me somewhere,
Settling in someone's breath is what
The age calls agreement

You dominate
My dreams and fantasies,
Losing senses in fits of passion is
What's called the heart's fascination

Incomplete dreams, fragmented notions ,
Life without shades and motions,
People here bill you as
Life's necessity

91.

Come along, let's go somewhere and build a home,
Narrate our stories to each other,
Voices will build the walls,
The roof will come from the good wishes

Silent lips will speak together,
Eyes of shyness will be enclosed within themselves,
The heart's chambers, vacant for years,
Will be your heart's abode

Sunrays, caressing your mellow lock of hair,
Will touch me,
The eastern breeze carrying your linen
In its carefree flow
Will fall within my unfolded arms

We will taste the slices of bliss,
Living together,
Watching each other for hours at stretch,
The sky will be our own and so will be
The moonlight,
Let's go, bring down the paradise on earth

We will lend tongue to feelings,
We will build a home of tender emotions,

We will found a settlement with
The world throbing inside,
We will embellish each city with
Umpteen Edens

92.

O Lord! Take some pity,
Make this world a bit more habitable

Hearths are not fuelled by blessings,
Make the blessings of the hungry a little more effective, credible

Dreams break everyday with the morning sun,
Make the dreams of the hapless a bit more believable

The world doesn't change overnight,
Make the thoughts of the oppressed a bit more dependable

The sun is a hostage of some tall mansions,
Make the light emitted by the glow-worms indomitable

Man is nothing but a picture of angst and hapless compulsion,
Make the impact of this truism a little more questionable

93.

I am a heart of glass, she a mansion of stone,
I don't know how to say that I have to love her

A sweet smell permeates my fancies,
I don't know how to say my arms have to seize her

I don't like coming and going like waves,
I don't know how to say I will melt when I merge with her

She is a charming beauty, the glow of the divine,
I don't know how to say I have to find my fortune in her

Grownup are those who are loving and caring,
I don't know how to say I have to make everyone a well-wisher

The world's eyes stand where your eyes stop,
I don't know how to say my eyes have to assimilate her

94.

Let me breathe in the open air to the backbone,
Let me cry too, I am not stone.

I know the world is not a paradise,
Let me wet my eyes today for some relations gone.

Just by wishing, a wish is not fulfilled,
For some dreams broken, let me bemoan.

Youth diverts with the coming of age,
Emotions extinct, let me collapse and scatter alone.

Cherishing someone in fancies doesn't secure a place in her heart,
If God be gracious, let me manage things on my own.

I have also read books about fairies,
Let me sleep soundly, and dream hover away like a barren drone.

Don't knock at the door to show up in my dream,
I am in peace, let my slumber go on

Fairies won't descend to accompany me in loneliness,
Let me find in dry faces relation trails to my isle of rubicon

95.

I have no trust in myself,
Nor do I trust you,
The heart is broken a bit,
The eyes are wet
To lead a life,
I have reared myriad illusions,
Some broken, some scattered,
Something is not complete yet

96.

I grayed moment by moment, pals
I became a time spent, pals

Everything got buried under a dune of sand,
Don't dig the ashes, pals

I watch the stars in bright, beautiful nights,
The moon has faded, pals

I have been kept preserved in a picture,
Don't embarrass me with reminiscences, pals

Sands disperse with the fist opening,
Don't access the frontiers of relationships, pals

97.

Quest for humans
Made me wander from one settlement to the other,
Some stones I found had become human and
Some humans were stone

Scrubbing off the gaudy crusts,
I came across corpses underneath,
I saw pictures guised as smiles
Cry and bemoan

Wine-house in the eve
Offered a different spectacle,
I found some earthen effigies weeping
Like the puerile and the undergrown

98.

In the ambiance of void, there would be smoke only,
Lots of people would be there, but the heart would be lonely

Crowd is thickening at the crossroads,
The path would now be more solitary

Now, there is hardly anything that looks fascinating,
The heart would be craving for a company

Man has discovered numerous means of death,
Life would find itself trapped in more difficulty

You have many naames in common parlance,
To say goodbye, would death ever pause for a jiffy?

99.

In this era,
It's not easy to smile at everything

When bruises come from your own brethren,
It's not easy to embrace, forgetting the suffering

They are coming to cuddle me with a knife hidden somewhere,
It's not easy to meet them laughing

Like weather, relations are sometimes nice and sometimes inclement,
It's not easy to maintain the string

I have also seen friendship and the world,
It's not easy to smile at everything

Everyone has his own way of living,
It's not easy to forget the silent nights sobbing

www.ingramcontent.com/pod-product-compliance
Lightning Source LLC
Chambersburg PA
CBHW070200100426
42743CB00013B/2988